How

Guid

FIRST STEPS

channeled from my
Spirit Guide
Angels

Book 1

by
LINDA DEIR

GUIDED ◁◉▷ Press

2675 W. Hwy 89A, PMB 1310,
Sedona, Arizona 86336
http://www.GuidedPress.com

Library of Congress Cataloging-in-Publication
Data
Deir, Linda; How to Live a Guided Life series,
FIRST STEPS, Book 1, channeled from my Spirit
Guide Angels is a compilation of channeled
insights that come through from Linda's *Spirit
Guide Angels* each week. These are the same *Spirit
Guide Angels* who have stood by Linda and guided
her since she was a baby. At the end of each insight
Linda explains: **HOW IT WORKS**

Editor: Ray Holley
Interior design and layout: Linda Deir
Cover design: Linda Deir

First Edition, 2015
ISBN# 13:978-0692457559 (Guided Press)

TABLE OF CONTENTS

Discovering who you are starts now

FOREWORD

NOTE: The use of italics.

 The italic text following this ICON are all the insights "channeled from my *Spirit Guide Angels*," including my reference to my *Spirit Guide Angels* throughout the book.

In this book, you will learn how to live a guided life. At any time along the way you can use this book as a reminder to keep you on your path before you stray too far off course. These reminders are your *spirit guide angels* catching you - before you slip and fall. *They* are always with you, there to catch you, and guide you...hence "Live a Guided Life."

What does it mean to Live a Guided Life?

- The struggle stops. Everyone is guided, not just once in awhile, but all the time. Where do you think all those great ideas come from? The ego would like you to think it comes from you. Being guided is not something you have to learn, it's what you need to learn to recognize when it shows up.
- When you acknowledge that you're being guided, your life becomes easier - a life that includes having some room in it, not one

that's maxed out, and all used up and spent. With the extra room you've made in your life, you learn to listen and spend some time alone so you're available to connect with your *guides*. That's when you begin to feel or hear *their* messages. It's a gentle knowing.

- If your life becomes difficult, that's your *guides* nudging you to make a course correction. Think of this as your *guides* holding up a big red stop sign.

- If you are motivated by fear then you are not listening to your *guides*. You are focused on the noise - those who are shouting at you because they have an agenda and are attempting to get you to do something that benefits them. Your *guides* have no agenda and *they* will never shout at you, that's how you know it's *them*.

What are the benefits of listening to your *Spirit Guide Angels* in the world today?

- Your *Guides* are the only ones who you can confide in about absolutely anything. *They* will never judge you, will always tell you the truth, while safeguarding your confidence. *They* don't care what you have or have not done in this lifetime. *Their* job is to provide guidance to you whenever you ask for it or are open to it.

- When you include your *Spirit Guide Angels*

your life becomes more fun and interesting. The struggle ends. It's a path that welcomes some alone time and quiet space and that may be the most challenging part for some because of family and other commitments. Shifting priorities around to make room for this new addition in your life will become imperative.

Facts - why this is the best time to start building a relationship with your *Spirit Guide Angels*.

- You will stop second-guessing yourself.
- Your struggles will end.

  Your *Guides* are always sending you clear communication. When you listen, you co-create a better life for yourself than you could have done on your own. When you learn to quiet your life, detecting *their* guidance becomes possible.

- As I mentioned before, your *guides* are always sending you signs and signals. Some of these are obstacles. *They* do this to get you back on course. When you're on the right track *they* provide smooth sailing. Your are always being guided!
- Their communication can take many forms. You may call it your intuition, good timing, luck, gut feelings, or you say things like, "I

knew that," or find yourself at the right place at the right time, or even say it came to you in a dream. Every one of these occurrences is how your *spirit guide angels* communicate with you. It comes directly from *them*. *They* send it "through you," "to you."

If a person is already doing well why do they need to build a relationship with their *Spirit Guide Angels*?

- Here's the test. What will these people do when their success takes a turn? Will they listen to the warning signs before any of this turns against them? Will they become a causality of this inconvenient change in their "luck?" If they get the warning signs will they trust them enough to know when or how to act on them? This can only come from an ongoing relationship with your *Spirit Guides*. as *they* guide you with perfect timing and you learn to detect and then act on *their* guidance, especially when the pressure is on.
- Real success involves much more than landing in a bed of roses every once in awhile. Many people can do that once, but real success is repeating it over and over again through all kinds of adversity and lessons along the way. This is where having

a relationship with your *Spirit Guides* will make you shine.

Chapter 1 - UNDERSTANDING YOURSELF COMES FIRST

Finding Your Way Home

"Do you ever doubt yourself, or second-guess yourself? This is a sign of low self-esteem. Why do you feel frustrated when this happens? It's because you know you can do better.

To do better, you must learn to think at a higher level. Are you stuck with people in your life who have low vibrational frequencies? Do you know why you like hanging out with them?

It's because you gravitated toward them in order to make yourself feel accepted, or one of the crowd. You lowered your standards.

You must surround yourself with people who are more spiritually aware. You will discover that this is the only way home."

HOW IT WORKS: Spending your time with superficial people leaves you feeling empty and worse than being alone. This message is telling you that you can do better, a lot better. If you insist on experiencing this then try to learn from it. Observe what these people are saying and doing. Don't engage, just observe. They may even judge you as stupid like you don't get it. Let that be their opinion as you continue to see things for what they really are. This is fail proof, it works every time, and it works quickly.

Slowing Down Your Life

"In order to hear us you must slow down your life. Find a quiet place and close your eyes.

Listen to your breathing, it is the rhythm of life. Once you are calm ask for our help - for it is in this calmness that our guidance comes through.

The constant noise and distractions going on all around you are what keeps you disconnected from us. We cannot shout over the noise in your life. To be effective, we must have your attention."

HOW IT WORKS: Consider all the "loudness" and the "shouting" that's going on all around you all the time. It's this shouting that you need to manage so you can begin to detect your *spirit guides*. Your *guides* respect you too much to ever shout at you. If it shouts at you, it's not your *guides*.

A Life Without Regret

"You must learn to choose without regret. The problem is that you have too many choices. So how do you know which one is without regret?

Look at the choices before you and examine which ones require compromise on your part. Either compromise in your values or a compromised lifestyle that you would have to lead.

It's the decisions that you make that require you to compromise that all lead to regrets at the end of your life.

We can help you make the right decisions."

HOW IT WORKS: Guilt is the culprit here. You are the judge of your better conduct, not someone else. Even if you make a poor decision, it's for you to learn from and do better next time. Guilt is designed to punish and your *guides* do not sanction that.

Making Quality Decisions

"People have great difficulty making quality decisions about their life. Two things happen; they either keep making the same decisions over and over again or the amount of stress in their life prevents them from giving enough of the right kind of thought to their important decisions.

That is why when we tell you - in order to learn who you are and why you are here, it takes releasing the stress you are under to get there. If you can't release the stress, you can't make a good decision because the stress is forcing you to decide one way or another.

When you connect with us, your Spirit Guides, we will show you how to release the stress so you can make clearer decisions through a pattern of clear decision-making. You will find out exactly who you are so you can learn to trust yourself."

HOW IT WORKS: Your *Spirit Guides* are acutely aware that to learn anything the environment for learning must first be established. The pressure that blocks learning must be released, and then *they* align you with what you are ready to experience at that particular moment. *They* trigger you with events that ignite your passions and set you on your journey. From all this, there's nothing you can't learn, figure out, do, or have. All you have to do is step into it.

Chapter 2 - LIMITATIONS AND HOW TO UNLEARN THEM

Change Evolves You Forward, Not Backward

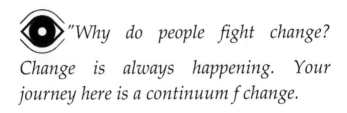*"Why do people fight change? Change is always happening. Your journey here is a continuum f change.*

You don't have to work on things in order to change. By working on them, you are, in fact, attempting to stop or manipulate change. Since change is constant you only have to adapt to it.

This is where we come in. Your life is a gift of change that you were sent here to experience. We guide you through that change even while you try to stop it or wish things were the way they were in the

*past. That's not how it works. Change
evolves you forward, not backward."*

HOW IT WORKS: Think of change as
new experiences. New experiences are fun
and exciting. Resistance to change is the
only thing that makes it hard. Like new
experiences, think of change like going on
vacation, to discover new people, places,
and things. This is the urge that brought
you here in the first place.

Why Would You Want To Change?

*"It's time for a change, at least
that's what people think. When it's New
Years people want to change something
about themselves or their life. What if you
can't change? What if your life is scripted
out ahead of time and you are just
experiencing it?*

Yes, people would like to not have setbacks, tragedies, or illnesses in their life. But what if they were all scripted into your journey? Rather than resisting change, why not just let the fearless person you are, the one you were before you got here, experience these changes? Rely on this person we're talking about because that's who you already are. That's the person who accepts these changes and faces them willingly.

When you get to the end of your journey here, everything you were concerned and worried about, or tried to change will disappear in an instant. What will be left? Your memories of a small child you helped, a garden you grew, a meal you fixed for yourself and loved ones that they appreciated. That's what you will remember. It's that you went on this journey and left the world with a little more love and compassion. You left the world a warmer place and you did it with our help.

Your greatest success was not what you did once you got here, but just in getting here. You had everything easy and difficult put in front of you as tests, as experiments that you get to learn from once you got here. So, desiring to change your life in any way would mean defeating the purpose in being here because that's what you came here to resolve within yourself."

HOW IT WORKS: Incarnating into a life is not as easy as you think. You and your *Spirit Guides* masterminded getting you here, and then *they* help you accomplish what you came here to do. However, once you arrived you were assigned your amnesia - forgetting most or all of what you intended to do once you arrived. You have the amnesia, not your *Spirit*

Guides. This is why you need to make a solid connection with *them.* The *one's* who walk with you faithfully.

Be Careful Of Why You Want Things

"What you want and how you are going to get it is much different than what you want and why you need it. This small distinction makes all the difference in your future and how abundance comes to you.

People say, "I want more money and I'll do anything necessary to get it." The fact that they've limited themselves to just wanting more money is the downfall in their strategy. Most people want more money, but why do you need it?

If you attach, "I want to buy a new car,"

or "I want to take a trip around the world" to what you want then that's shallow. You may, or may not get what you want even though you're willing to anything to get it.

The "why" part needs to be something that makes you a better person. For example, "I want more money so I can support my favorite charity, or I want to put it into my passion that will help the world in some great way" This is the small difference that makes all the difference."

HOW IT WORKS: Stuff only allows you to rent temporary pleasure. Wanting stuff is a reaction to filling a void. It's like putting a Band-Aid on a fatal wound. You didn't come here to have stuff, you came here to heal and learn. You came here to become more than you were before you got here. This is what you take with you when you are released from this life, not the stuff.

A Lifetime Of Learned Limitations

"What does it take to make a lifelong connection with us? We will tell you that first you must clear your mind of a lifetime of learned limitations.

Children come into this world perfect and open. They're here to learn, but people teach them the wrong things. Instead of being allowed to grow up as the person they came in as - they are told who they should be. They are told what to think, what to believe, who to love, and how to live.

These life limitations creep into their lives

16

one-by-one until they are not the same person who originally showed up."

HOW IT WORKS: You need to think like a baby, a new person, the real you. Here's how you start...follow your curiosities. Imagine doing this in spite of all the existing demands and obligations you have as an adult. Make some room in your life, creating "a time out," to play with some of your curiosities. That's your guidance coming through - your compass. These curiosities are being sent to you directly from your *guides,* that's because *they* know what's really important to you.

Chapter 3 - EMOTIONS YOU CAN TRUST

Truth and Love Are The Same

"We will never lie to you because we love you. To us, truth and love are the same.

It's difficult to lie to someone you love and even more difficult to love someone who lies to you. We are not saying that the truth is always easy. It can be painful or joyous.

When you compromise a relationship by lying you eat away at the foundation of that relationship until there's nothing left and it crumbles.

You must always tell the truth. When you tell the truth you are the truth - you are love."

HOW IT WORKS: If you have to lie this is a sign from the most authentic part of yourself that you are around the wrong people and situations. Granted, there are a lot of wrong people and situations out there. You attract your *spirit guides* to you by living a truthful, loving life. This prevents you from ever second-guessing yourself.

You Don't Get To Choose Who Loves You

"We are relationship experts. We have provided you with all the relationships you've ever had in this life. You may say, "Why did you give me some that were painful, or didn't work out?" It's because of your need to learn and become a whole person.*

When you were young we provided the events, occurrences, people, and thoughts to you - so that you selected a specific relationship. When you were young these relationships were to be learning experiences for you. You went through several before you finally realized what you didn't want in a relationship. You had to go through them in order to find this out. It was you who changed, and not necessarily the other person.

Now that you've had a few relationships you have a well-defined list of what you want. However, this list is something that you expect. We will tell you that your best relationship to come is something you don't expect. It will show up right in front of you as soon as you lose your list."

HOW IT WORKS: The message in this guidance is that you can't chase a relationship. That's what *they* meant by *"losing your list."* When you do this you remove yourself from doing the picking. This is powerful because now you are no longer blocking that perfect relationship. Expecting nothing will produce miracles.

Who Are You Hanging Out With?

"Who are you hanging out with? What are they doing to you? What have they got you believing in? What are they getting you to say? Which direction do they have you moving in?

Better yet, what do they have you becoming? Ask yourself if all the above is okay?

We've noticed that butterflies never hang out with caterpillars. That's because they've changed. They no longer need the solitary confinement of being a caterpillar. Once they've become a butterfly they've changed forever.

So, don't get stuck trying to go back to your past. Ask us for guidance. Ask us to help you change."

HOW IT WORKS: If the people in your life do not want you to change or learn new things, or try new things - they will keep you in solitary confinement, like the confinement of being the caterpillar. That's not love. Love is feeling loved and that only happens when you are loved and appreciated for who you are, not for what someone needs you to be.

22

Jealousy is Caused by Low Self-Esteem

"What is it that you desire? If you desire things for yourself you can develop feelings of disappointment and lack. People usually desire physical things that they don't have that others do. So they desire to be like someone else who has made a good life for themselves. Either way, you are jealous of them.

If you desire things for others you raise your vibrational frequency level and this is in the sense of helping someone, or hoping that they get what they need. This is not jealousy, although it is desiring.

If you desire things for yourself you are operating in lower vibrational frequencies and over time you just become more stuck in the illusion of the psychical existence *that you are experiencing in this lifetime.*

So, while it's okay to desire, be careful of what it is you desire or obsess over. If you find yourself only desiring things for yourself that you don't get, it can only lead to jealousy."

HOW IT WORKS: Jealousy makes you aware that you have been living a compromised life. The opposite of jealousy is living a passionate, meaningful life. Jealous people are seeing something they desire and get angry because they don't have it. In reality, most times what they desire they would not want if they realized what it took to get it. Jealousy reeks with self-centeredness and insecurity. It brings out the worst in people.

Chapter 4 - EXPANSION INTO THE REAL YOU

We Teach You Differently

"Where do you go to get your education? Traditionally people went to a formal educational institution. You can seek out your education for a long time. You can learn a lot about one thing or a little about many things, it depends on what you intend to do with it. If you know a lot about one thing you can become a teacher or expert in that field.

We teach you differently. You must have the knowledge and that's what you get with formal training and education. We teach wisdom, which is very different.

You could go outside and look around

and, if you have an education, you could describe everything you see. But, when you have wisdom, you can look around and describe everything you can't see. There is a great difference, but you need both. You can't be heavy in one and light in another - you must strike a balance and that's what we guide you to do. You may have the knowledge to play the piano, but without the wisdom you can't feel the music."

HOW IT WORKS: This is what it feels like when you live in two worlds simultaneously. It's a blend of the magical and practical. You see people who are really good at one or the other, but that's no longer good enough. To give the world what they are truly yearning for you need to express your knowledge and wisdom by being authentic, novel, and daring. The important things are the hardest to say, they are like landmarks to a treasure that are uniquely yours and only you can convey.

Having An Intentional Mind

"Most people know about the importance of "now." There's been the "power of now" and "living in the present moment" and much more written about it. We look at it differently.

We see that there will never be another now. Here's the problem with all that's been taught. Thinking about, or meditating on the "now" by trying to clear your mind and concentrate on it only removes you from the experience.

Being present in the now doesn't mean

28

an empty mind. Being present in the now means having an intentional mind. There is no place for you to go in this life. There is only a place to be at any moment. There is only where you are and what you are doing. You have already arrived."

HOW IT WORKS: When you live your life from intention you know who you are. When you know yourself, you trust yourself. Living an intentional life is what it takes to overcome anything that stands in the way of a safe, okay life versus a meaningful one. This is the power of the intentional mind.

Your Soul's First Responders

"We are puzzled about how you treat us. Most of the time, you treat us like a last resort, or your spiritual spare

tire, when we should be your steering wheel.

It hurts you when you don't come to us first. We are always with you and available, but you go out and ask everybody else for help.

You pray for something to show up in your life, when we could show you how to get it.

Many times we see praying as spiritual begging and it's not proactive.
We are your Soul's First Responders and are at the scene when you need us. Try asking us for help first and see how much your life changes."

HOW IT WORKS: Imagine having the best *life coaches* at your disposal whenever you need *them*. *They* don't even charge you anything for this most qualified advice.

They safeguard your confidence, have no personal agenda, and are completely unbiased. That just begins to describe your *spirit guides*.

Your Beliefs Are Formed By Events

"Are you happy or unhappy because of the way life treats you? What do life's events mean to you? Your life is controlled by your inner responses to these outer events.

People respond differently to the same event. For example, thousands of people watching the same sporting event. Half go home happy because their team won. The other half is sad because their team lost. They both witnessed the same event.

31

Events and how you react to them compose your beliefs about life's limitations or possibilities. Happiness is produced by the mind. Allow us to take charge of your mind to direct you toward happiness. We can positively impact how your life unfolds."

HOW IT WORKS: Here's how it works – you become an observer. When you become the observer you stop taking everything personally. This is when you start to see the possibilities your *guides* are showing you. It's also when *they* chime in.

Understanding Your Personal Power

"Let's talk about personal power. Everybody has it, but everyone expresses it differently. Some people express it as a great teacher, or artist, or craftsman, or

thinker, or inventor.

We see it all coming from a calm and intentional conviction inside the person. This deep down power source center is what causes you to act in a certain way. The ability to follow your path with conviction is necessary even if it's not convenient at the time, or if you would rather be doing something else.

Personal power doesn't have to be forceful at all because it comes from a place inside where there is no fear. It doesn't require that you be rewarded for this power because it's your soul's intention to deliver this power to the world regardless. This power doesn't have to attack others because that just turns into domination and people will resent you for that.

Personal power doesn't require any kind of force to be delivered - it only requires love."

HOW IT WORKS: Think of your personal power as being in the zone. That's your sweet spot and it's how you attract your *guides*. The mix between the being in the zone and tapping into the intelligent foresight of your *guides* makes you unstoppable. This is the highest way of living your life because everything is instantly available to you. It also sets a great example for others to observe and live by. It's contagious.

Chapter 5 - LISTENING AND HEARING YOUR GUIDES

Listen With Your Heart

"*To hear us you must listen. To listen, you must be silent. You never learn anything by speaking. When you listen in silent receptivity you can change your life.*

You must listen over the constant noise of your surroundings. Once you can reach the silence you can hear us.

Listen to us with your heart so we can touch your soul. The silence is what makes it happen."

HOW IT WORKS: *They* just described two levels of listening. One is listening in silent receptivity and the other is listening with your heart. They are both listening. Receptivity creates the environment for listening. Listening with your heart is the fastest and highest form of listening. Master the listening - the two-way communication with your *guides* will come next.

To Hear Us, You Must Be Available

"*What good is getting advice or guidance if you are not listening? You aren't paying us money to advise you, but you should at least be open when we speak to you.*

You must be available in order for us to reach you. Now, by being available we mean being present, and listening for our guidance, and expecting it to come to you at any time. The way you do this is to not become so distracted by the things in your life. That's what consumes you, preventing our guidance from reaching you.

Think of us as always broadcasting messages, like a radio you never turn off. It's always going on in the background. Unlike broadcasted music that you turn on to entertain you or to help you make it through the day - our messages can change your day.

So, each day several times during the day stop and take a breath and ask yourself, "Am I still listening, or do I need to slow down and become more aware and available?"

HOW IT WORKS: Like hitting a reset button, check in with yourself throughout the day to detect your level of awareness.

In the instant you do this, all the distractions and noises will become louder. They didn't change in volume, your awareness became sharper, hence everything is instantly enhanced. Like tuning a radio - you just tuned out the distractions and noise and tuned into your guidance.

We Broadcast 24 Hours a Day

"People pick up on our guidance but do so sporadically - an idea here, a hunch there, but most of the time people miss out on where it's coming from.

We can tell you that we are always sending you communication and guidance. For example; the ideas you get in the shower come from us, all those hunches and gut feelings are all forms of communication from us. How about telepathy? That's our favorite way of sending guidance, but we also do it in dreams and the times just before you go to sleep and right after you wake up. We send you guidance while you're driving and while you're at work.

We send you messages, lessons, and experiences all the time. It's just that people have a hard time believing that all this is coming from us. Start writing down the guidance you receive as you receive it.

Also, remember that our guidance has a shelf-life. You can think about it and decide how it feels in your life, but you must act on it while it's still fresh. Looking back on your journal of guidance you will be surprised how many messages you get from us each day."

HOW IT WORKS: Telepathy is the way your *Spirit Guides* communicate with *each other*. It's *their* communication of choice when communicating with you, however, you are more likely to miss it. That's why *they* send you signs and signals, hunches and nudges - these are more obvious to you. Learning *their* language of communication is vital to your well-being.

Chapter 6 - ACCEPTANCE HAPPENS WHEN THE BLAME STOPS

The Present Time is Eternity

"Everybody seems to say, "Focus on the present." You can't change the past or worry about the future, you can only act in the present. The present is really eternity because if you can only act in the present then there is no time.

People can't wish they had more time because there is no such thing. We do not operate in the constriction of your time-based existence.

We are always available to help you in the present. The present is always your doorway to reaching us."

HOW IT WORKS: Eternity exists where

you are right now. So, what's eternity? It's living with intention and purpose - every step of the way. Wishing you had more time means you are serving time and not living a life of intention and purpose. Don't bother living any other way because you didn't come here to serve time, you came here to accomplish your mission - live an intentional, purposeful life. This is where your *guides* reside.

Who Is It You Are Chasing?

"*On the road to enlightenment two things are happening. One is what you already possess, and the other is the unobtainable illusions that you are chasing. These are the imaginary pleasures you seek.*

What if you are what you are supposed to

discover? What if you are the destination that you're seeking? Suppose that trying to find your way is really losing yourself? That you may be getting further and further away from yourself and from us.

The sooner you learn that the person in the mirror is who you are supposed to be your pain will stop and you will start to love that person with our help."

HOW IT WORKS: Are you critical of that person you see in the mirror? Once you are released from this perceived notion of yourself your *guides* can begin to reach you. The "mirror" is symbolic of illusions.

A Life of Consequences

"You were born into a life of consequences. Everyone who chooses to

incarnate accepts these consequences before they get here.

These consequences can be as different as being born with a silver spoon in your mouth, or being born into abject poverty. Both existences have consequences that must be recognized and faced before a person discovers who they are and why they came here. Both people in these examples will go through life with a desire, an urge, to find the answers to those most important questions of who they are and why they're here. It is not diffcult or easier for either person. It is many times a lifetime of struggle to discover something that deep inside they know is there. That's because before they got here it was always there.

It's the 'before life' you came from that implants this urge deep inside you to discover yourself. People, however, spend their lifetime chasing things they believe will make them who they are - when who they really are they brought with them on that very first day here."

HOW IT WORKS: Consequences are the price of being here. Knowing this, you can remove a lot of confusion about your choices because there will be consequences, when both good or bad things happen. Your choices are loaded with consequences, whether you make them or let someone make them for you. When you are prepared to face what shows up - you should expect consequences. Don't let that scare you! With this all sorted out you can get to know who you are and why you're here without feeling guilty about the inevitable consequences.

Stop Resisting the Natural Flow

"*People fear accepting what they are doing. They fight the natural flow. This puts them "off-center." Being off-center means the inability to center themselves.*

What is happening around them is change. People say that change is the only constant. The universe is always in a state of growth and flux.

Fighting or resisting growth means you will never free yourself from being controlled by change. Your life only becomes favorable when you stop resisting and learn to adapt.

We can help you with this - walk with us."

HOW IT WORKS: I know what *they*

meant when they said, *"Resisting growth means you will never free yourself from being **controlled** by change*." I learned this just before I turned two years old. It was then when I was out of options. That's when I stopped struggling with the dilemma I found myself in – and a profound awareness came to me when I stopped resisting the natural flow. That's when my *Spirit Guides* came into focus (chapter 2 of my book, <u>GUIDED</u>)

Chapter 7 - AWARENESS WILL END THE STRUGGLE

The Paths to Enlightenment

"*Your path to enlightenment began with you having a restless feeling. This feeling was one of something lacking in your life, but you didn't know what it was.*

So, you went down many paths to seek answers and most were dead ends, which brought you right back to where you started. What really was happening as you reached the dead ends and returned to the beginning of your path is you were being shown what you were seeking was the home where you came from, where you started.

We came with you on this life journey and watched you get lost. We are called your

"Spirit Guide Angels" for a reason, as we provide the guidance to you to get you home, where you began, so you can successfully navigate this journey. This is where you began before you started looking."

HOW IT WORKS: There are no secrets, no gurus that have your answers, no holy grail – only you have your answers. Seeking answers did not satisfy you because they were not yours. No wonder you kept looking. That's the good news. Now that you realize all the time you've wasted, here's your shortcut, return to *"where you began before you started looking."* That's where you will find yourself and uncover your purpose.

Make This Life Your Best Life

"Are you one of those people who believes that if a good person suffers in this lifetime they will get their reward in heaven? And, when you see bad people, corrupt people, who have everything - do you believe that they will also get their punishment after this life by burning in the eternal fires of hell?

If you hold on to this judgment you are missing a chance to be rewarded in this life. When you abandon this type of thinking and follow our guidance you will not have to struggle in this life waiting for some future reward.

You will discover that by following our guidance you get rewarded every day. Your life will become less stressful and once that happens you will be able to make clearer decisions. Making better decisions leads to better outcomes immediately.

Why wait to get some 'down the road' reward when you can improve your everyday life in many ways just by following our guidance?"

HOW IT WORKS: There is no justification for struggling in your life. When you walk with your *guides* your life becomes a fascinating adventure. It's so good and so right that it feels like you are cheating. It only feels that way because everyone else is struggling. People resent you for making decisions that liberate you. They have excuses for not making better decisions as they continue to create a life of needless struggle.

Ask For Abundance Not Excess Abundance

"Everyone says, "I want more." Think about what that means.

You use the Law of Attraction in an attempt to manifest what you want and more of what you already have. Do you think that the Universe wants you to become more materialistic? Or, does the Universe want you to have just a sufficient amount of abundance?

You don't need abundance in excess. If you ask for excessive abundance that isn't abundance, that's a distraction. The Universe will give you what you need, but you will pay dearly for excesses."

HOW IT WORKS: If you can't take it with you - it's an illusion. Why ask for the illusion when you can have the real thing? YOU are the real thing. Have fun discovering what that is as you expand and explore what your *guides* are placing on your path.

Discovering Who You Are Starts Now

"People seem very concerned with how they've lived their lives in the past and imagining how they will live their lives in the future. All this time spent reflecting and projecting only causes the person to lose their focus in life now in the present.

You can't go back and change anything you've done. Nor can you feel what it's like to live your life like you imagine it may turn out in the future.

Here's an exercise to help you live in the present. Go to a quite place, maybe in the woods or just outside. Now, using all your senses describe ten or more things that are happening.

What do you feel - do you feel a warm breeze? What do you see - do you see dew on the leaves? Do you smell grass after a rain? Is that an airplane flying over? What kind of birds were those that just flew by singing?

Once you can start describing everything that's going on around you - you will start to see what it takes to live in the present moment. Living in the present moment is imperative in order for you to discover yourself."

HOW IT WORKS: Your *guides* are asking

you to remove the distractions, the "should dos," and any hopelessness you are holding onto. *They* know that when you let it work - it does. That's when you start to breathe and release the pressure. Until that happens your *guides* can't reach you.

Chapter 8 - FEARS APPEAR WHEN YOU FORGET WHO YOU ARE

Fears Are What Keep You Stuck Here

"Everything keeping you stuck is based in fear. Fear about your job, your personal worth, not having enough possessions, fear about relationships, your appearance, money, and much more.

We reside in higher vibrational realms and we do not have all these fears. By associating with us, we will show you how not to live in fear.

If you continue to indulge in these fears, you will remain stuck in a lower vibrational existence that will interfere with your ability to find clarity and ascend.

You will find yourself being pulled back into another incarnate existence until you get it right."

HOW IT WORKS: You become like those you associate with. Like superheroes, your *guides* are fearless intelligent *beings.* Associating with *them* will not only prevent you from living a life of struggling, you will, by association, become more like *them.*

Why People Fear Dying

"Why do people fear dying? Mostly it's because they haven't yet learned how to live. It starts with your first breath.

You don't fear coming into this life, you embrace it. You choose it anticipating the possibilities of living a fulfilling life. With your first breath, you breathe in choices.

With that first breath, you think okay, "I'm here, now what do I choose to do at this moment and the next?" This is where you can get off track. Are you listening to yourself or to others? Why would you listen to others tell you who to be, what to do, what to buy, or who to love?

From that first breath you must learn to know yourself, so you can be you throughout your life. It's not too late to learn to breathe."

HOW IT WORKS: Knowing who you are is the foundation upon which you create your entire life. It is the critical first step. If you missed it your *guides* are recommending that you start from the beginning by using your breath. This will release the pressure in your life so your *guides* can reach you and *they* can show you the way back to yourself.

Never Label Events as Good or Bad

👁 *"How do you feel about accidents? Do you think that everything happens for a reason or a purpose and there are no accidents?*

Everything that happens is an event and it's presented to you as an opportunity to learn. However, your mind tends to label these events as being either, good or bad.

The good ones are things like good fortune or luck and they happen "for you." The ones labeled bad are things that happen "to you," like a tragedy or some kind of problem.

Now, many people who have had a great stroke of luck or fortune, have won the lottery, and for many it destroyed their lives. Other events labeled as bad that happened to you could have been an accident of some kind that hurt you. Yet it was through that challenge you found purpose in your life; so you weren't a victim after all. Never label events, only learn from them."

HOW IT WORKS: Good or bad is a strong perception. It's all because of social conditioning. The truth is that nothing ever happens to you, everything happens for you. You are given these events to teach you what you intended to learn before you came here. This is the intention of your soul.

Living A Fear Based Life

"How do you know when you are living in fear? We see you cowering from important decisions that would change

your life for the better.

You have trouble making the important decisions because you fear retaliation from your spouse, or family, or boss, or children. You are afraid of what everybody will think, or do.

If you continue this pattern you will only increase the pain in your life and find yourself making decisions through compromise, which only leads to regrets.

When it comes to important decisions just ask us and avoid the fear."

HOW IT WORKS: Fear stops people from experiencing new things and believing in themselves. These are the two things your *guides* value the most in you. In fact, when you have a relationship with your *guides* this cannot happen to you.

Thinking Is Really Worrying

"Do you think that man's greatest ability, being so evolved, is the ability to think? We don't. We see that the more a person thinks the more they worry. Thinking about your future is really worrying about it.

We see man's greatest ability as the ability to listen. When you listen you're not worrying. In order to listen and hear us you must first stop, slow down and breathe. Clear your mind of thinking and worrying. Open up to receiving everything we tell you. You must be present, or actively aware. This makes you receptive.

Now, once in this receptive mode, start asking your questions. Ask them one at a *time and do not ask complex questions. Focus on just one issue in your life. Then listen for our response as it will come right away.*

Once you have our answer, then ask your next question. By using this method and perfecting it you will find that we are available at all times. So, stop thinking and worrying and just start listening."

HOW IT WORKS: The goal of listening is to detect what your *spirit guides* are always showing you. *They* are "on" 24/7 every day of your life. *They* are there to help you. *They* know everything about you. *They* are your biggest fans. Most of all, *they* believe in you and know exactly why you are here and what you intend to accomplish. Give up the over-thinking and worrying about everything – just listen.

Worry is Self-Abuse

"We would like to talk to you about worry. Worry is a troubled state of mind. We call it self-abuse. If someone told you every day you had to worry you would accuse them of abusing you. So why do you do it to yourself?

Worry leads to pharmaceutical drugs to treat things like depression, anxiety, and addressing what you think is wrong with you. Worry is self-generated, it's your choice. You choose to worry.

You worry because you take things personally. You must create a space between yourself and your reactions to things. That's where we can enter. Stop reacting and give us a chance to reach you. Just step back, breathe, and listen."

HOW IT WORKS: Worry freezes you up.

Worrying is so consuming that when it starts it completely dominates you until there is no YOU. It's like a prison that you put yourself into, the penalty box. This is why *they* named it self-abuse. This is a behavior that leads to sickness. So create that space *they* talked about that lets your *Guides* help you move beyond this limitation and into your true nature.

About The Author

For Linda Deir living a guided life "is" her life.

Right from the start, she met her *spirit guides*. She was just a baby when it began. Having never been separated from *them, they* have guided her through unimaginable circumstances, as well as her greatest successes and understandings of herself.

Throughout her life, she has followed *their* guidance and accomplished what others considered impossible. From her lifelong relationship with her *spirit guide angels*, she knows firsthand that there's nothing you can't learn, figure out, do, or have when you live a guided life.

In a world that requires people to look for answers in unconventional ways, this has never been unconventional to Linda. Her many achievements are proof that when you co-create your life with your *guides*, hence, live a guided life, you can accomplished anything. All you need to do is show up, pay attention, listen, and take action.

From the training that started as a baby, she mastered living in two worlds simultaneously. What everyone in this life taught her, paled in comparison to what she learned from her *guides*.

Your *guides* don't teach you anything. *They* present you with timely events and opportunities that entice you. *They* have timing down to a science! So anything that excites you is always being sent directly from your *guides*, not just once in awhile, but all the time. This means that everything you receive has a shelf-life. *Their* timely guidance only works if you take action without hesitating. This is the most challenge part of following *their* guidance and will be critical to your success and learning. So when you feel that curiosity and wonder hit you, igniting your passions, you will know it's coming directly from your *spirit guide angels*.

The channeled insights presented in this book are *their* attempt to clear the path for you to make contact with your own *guides*. *They* show you how to incorporate *their* guidance into your life, creating a better life for yourself than you could have done on your own.

When *they* observe that you acted on *their* timely guidance you become a *spirit guide* magnet as *they* are attracted to the real you in action! Linda calls this the zone. You become unstoppable when you make this connection to your *source connected spirit guide angels*. Living a guided life is like stepping onto your very own yellow brick road as you connect the dots in your own life. Everything begins to make sense when you live a guided life. Let *their* messages bring you the power and clarity to make great decisions and live a fear-free life.

Linda and her husband and business partner, Ray Holley, channel these insights from Linda's *Spirit Guide Angels*, the same way they perform all their services on their other websites: www.channeledreadings.com and news.channeledreadings.com

A Note from Linda Deir

Thank you so much for reading How to Live a Guided Life, FIRST STEPS, Book 1, channeled from my *Spirit Guide Angels*.

Pay it forward by writing a short, helpful review of this book if it helped you or at least entertained you. Now you can help others. It will only take a few minutes of your time. Do that by going to Amazon (you did not need to buy the book on Amazon to leave a review). Type "How to Live a Guided Life, FIRST STEPS, Book 1, channeled from my *Spirit Guide Angels* by Linda Deir" into the search field. Go down to "Write a customer review" click on it and follow the fun part of writing your review and rating it by clicking the stars.

Get new insights on How to Live a Guided Life channeled from my *Spirit Guide Angels* delivered to your email box each Tuesday. Sign up at Linda's website: www.LindaDeir.com then click on the navigation bar at the top of the page that says: Linda's Weekly "Guided" Insights (http://lindadeir.com/sign-up-to-lindas-weekly-guided-insights/) ~ Linda Deir

Linda's Other Books

(All of my books are available on Amazon, Audible and iTunes in papaerback, Kindle and autobook formats)

GUIDED - Her Spirit Guide Angels Were Her Best Friends and Life Coaches

GUIDED is the author's true story that follows her life from survival as an abused child through her escape as a teenager and into her phenomenal success as a businesswoman in a man's world by age 19 and beyond. Using her life as a template, GUIDED is a roadmap for stepping on board at any point along your life path to join forces with your own *spirit guides* to create a better life than you could have on your own. Sprinkled throughout the book are 137 universally applicable Tips, Lessons, and Awarenesses that Linda shares directly from her life-long relationship with her *spirit guides*.

Printed in Great Britain
by Amazon.co.uk, Ltd.,
Marston Gate.